I0794244

# AP® English Language Skills Practice Workbook

*to accompany*

## Ideas in Argument

### Building Skills and Understanding

for the AP® English Language Course

John Williamson
Model Laboratory School at Eastern Kentucky University, KY

Mary Jo Zell
Keller High School, TX

Elizabeth Davis
College Station High School, TX

bedford, freeman & worth publishers

ISBN-13: 978-1-319-47189-7

Third Printing

Printed in the United States of America

Bedford, Freeman & Worth Publishers
120 Broadway
Floor 25
New York, NY 10271
bfwpub.com/high-school/us

*Table of Contents*

# UNIT 1
# Communicating an Idea

**Creating a Message (p. 6)**

Think of a situation where you are trying to convince or persuade someone. Describe your message. Consider your subject, perspective, and unifying idea.

| | |
|---|---|
| **Subject**<br>What is the literal subject? | |
| **Perspective**<br>What is your position on the subject? | |
| **Unifying Idea**<br>What larger idea are you advancing about the subject? | |
| **Message** | |

**Describing the Rhetorical Situation (p. 7)**

As you read, use the following graphic organizer to identify and describe the components of the rhetorical situation. You'll be asked to consider how the components influence the writer's message.

| Describing the Rhetorical Situation | | |
|---|---|---|
| **Component** | **Questions for Consideration** | **Significance for This Text** |
| Writer (or Speaker) | Who is the writer?<br><br>What is his or her role?<br><br>What values and beliefs does the writer hold about the subject?<br><br>What is the writer's relationship to both the situation and the audience? | |
| Context | In what circumstance was this text created?<br><br>What is going on historically? Politically? Socially? Culturally? | |
| Exigence | What is the writer's relationship to the context?<br><br>What has motivated the writer to create this text? | |
| Audience | Whom is the writer addressing in this text?<br><br>What is that audience's background? How do they likely feel about the subject? | |
| Purpose | Why did the writer create this text for this audience? What is he or she trying to do? | |
| Message | What is the writer's message for this audience? | |

## Developing a Claim (p. 12)

Consider a subject such as pets, music, or video games. Craft a thesis statement that contains a claim (perspective and idea) and takes a position.

| Thesis Statement | | |
|---|---|---|
| **Subject** | **Claim**<br>**Perspective + Unifying Idea** | |
| | | |

**Describing the Thesis of an Argument (p. 13)**

As you read the following essay by Stephen King, look for his thesis statement. Identify the subject and his claim (both the perspective and the idea). Record the different types of evidence King uses to defend his overall argument.

| Identifying Thesis and Supporting Evidence | | |
|---|---|---|
| **Subject** | **Claim**<br><br>**Perspective + Unifying Idea** | |
| | | |
| | **Evidence** | |
| | | |

**Analyzing the Narrative (p. 19)**

Think of a movie or streamed show that you've seen recently. Use the organizer that follows to record the arc of the story and elements of the story line. Then identify specific or concrete details associated with the three aspects of the narrative. Describe how these details could take on a larger symbolic or figurative meaning.

| **Analyzing Narrative Structure** | | |
|---|---|---|
| | **Questions to Ask** | **Concrete Details and Their Figurative Meaning** |
| **The Set-Up (Beginning)** | Who is telling the story?<br><br>What details establish the problem, tension, or conflict? | |
| **The Blow-Up (Middle)** | What are the values or ideas represented by each side of the conflict? | |
| **The Wrap-Up (End)** | How is the conflict resolved?<br><br>What does the narrator come to realize? | |

**Analyzing a Narrative (p. 20)**

As you read Gary Soto's personal narrative, "The Jacket," use the graphic organizer that follows to record details of the story that will help you understand his message. The details of the story should help you discover what Soto comes to realize because of his experience. How is this idea relevant to people other than Soto?

| **Analyzing Narrative Structure** | | |
|---|---|---|
| | **Questions to Ask** | **Concrete Details and Their Figurative Meaning** |
| **The Set-Up (Beginning)** | Who is telling the story?<br><br>What details establish the problem, tension, or conflict? | |
| **The Blow-Up (Middle)** | What are the values or ideas represented by each side of the conflict? | |
| **The Wrap-Up (End)** | How is the conflict resolved?<br><br>What does the narrator come to realize? | |

## Using Precise Diction (p. 26)

Choose an emotion, such as happy, sad, or scared, and create a tonal scale of at least three words for that emotion from least intense to most intense. Then draw or pick an emoji for each of the words.

| Least Intense | | Most Intense |
|---|---|---|
| | | |

**Describing Tone (p. 27)**

As you read the narrative, identify where Noah's tone shifts. Create a table illustrating Noah's diction before and after this shift. How does Noah's diction reveal a shift in tone? Considering his shift in tone, what is his overall claim?

| Identifying Shifts in Tone | |
|---|---|
| **Words before the Shift** | **Words after the Shift** |
| | |
| **Tone Before** → | **Tone After** |
| ↓ | |
| **Claim** | |
| | |

## Creating a Message (p. 65)

Reflect on moments in your life that resulted in a new understanding and then choose a unifying idea and perspective and draft the message that you want to communicate in your narrative. For example, in Brighton Earley's narrative, she recounts her experiences with shopping at Chevron to communicate that flexibility helped her overcome her difficulties.

If you are having trouble getting started, try to recall moments in your life when you had the following experiences, which often lead to new insights:

- You learned a new skill.
- You had a thrilling adventure.
- You lost a family member or friend.
- You made a new friend.
- You overcame a fear.

Just remember that your message and your narrative account of the experience must align.

| Message with Unifying Idea | Related Experiences |
|---|---|
| | |

**Establishing a Unifying Idea (p. 66)**

1. Using your message from the previous activity, identify your unifying idea.
2. Record details and notes from your experience in the proper column. Notes should contain both events and reflections on the events.

| **Message:** | | |
|---|---|---|
| **Unifying Idea:** | | |
| **The Set-Up (Beginning)** | **The Blow-Up (Middle)** | **The Wrap-Up (End)** |
| | | |

**Developing and Supporting a Thesis (p. 68)**

As you continue the process, review the message and unifying idea that you wish to convey to your audience, along with the notes about your pivotal moment that you brainstormed on page 66.

Write a thesis that includes your idea and message on a subject.

Record details that are relevant to your unifying idea and message, which you can use as evidence.

<table>
<tr><th colspan="3">Identifying Thesis and Supporting Evidence</th></tr>
<tr><th>Subject</th><th colspan="2"><u>Claim</u><br><br>Perspective + Unifying Idea</th></tr>
<tr><td rowspan="3"></td><td></td><td></td></tr>
<tr><th colspan="2">Evidence</th></tr>
<tr><td></td><td></td></tr>
</table>

**Revising and Editing a Narrative (p. 69)**

| Peer Revision Checklist: Revising and Editing a Narrative | | |
|---|---|---|
| **Questions to Consider** | **Unit One Focus Skills** | **Comment on the Effectiveness and/or Make a Suggestion** |
| Does the claim in the introduction or conclusion convey the writer's message and connect it to an idea that serves to unify the narrative? | *Narrative* | |
| Are the details of the narrative arranged in an appropriate order for the audience? | *Details connected to idea* | |
| Are all the details the writer included relevant to the unifying idea?<br><br>Do the details in the story lead to insight and reflection that convey a deeper understanding of the idea? | *Message* | |
| Has the writer crafted the narrative with effective diction that conveys the writer's tone and attitude? | *Diction for attitude connotation/ denotation* | |
| Is the writing free of errors in spelling, punctuation, capitalization, and other writing conventions? | *Punctuating syntactical features* | |

# UNIT 2
# Appealing to an Audience

*Ideas in Argument*, 1e

**Rhetorical Appeals (p. 87)**

| Rhetorical Appeals | | |
|---|---|---|
| **Appeal** | **Rhetorical Effect** | **Common Techniques** |
| **Pathos** – Appeal to Emotion | When writers pull on the heartstrings of their audience, they are attempting to persuade them by engaging some aspect of the audience's emotions or senses. When persuading, writers attempt to move an audience toward a specific action or belief. | Allusions<br>Anecdote<br>Connotations<br>Examples<br>Figurative language<br>Imagery<br>Repetition<br>Sensory details |
| **Logos** – Appeal to Logic | Appeals to logos engage the audience's sense of reasoning or logic, attempting to rationalize his or her perspective or idea to the audience.<br><br>Writers appeal to logos by making clear, detailed arguments. | Allusions<br>Analogies<br>Anecdote<br>Charts<br>Examples<br>Expert sources<br>Facts<br>Graphs<br>Statistics<br>Personal testimony<br>Repetition<br>Research<br>Syntax |
| **Ethos** – Appeal to Credibility | A strong ethical appeal can build rapport and earn the trust of an audience. A writer's background, character, status/position, or association are all means by which he or she implicitly attempts to persuade the audience of his or her credibility. Writers can also associate themselves with the audience by highlighting shared values. | Concession<br>Facts<br>Personal testimony<br>Refutation<br>Statistics<br>Sincerity<br>Use of credible and reliable sources<br>Writer's authority and experience |

**Appealing to an Audience (p. 88)**

Consider a rhetorical situation (like the curfew example at the beginning of this unit) you have experienced. Now, analyze your intended audience, considering their background, beliefs, and values. What rhetorical choices would you make to achieve your goal with that audience? How would you attempt to appeal to them?

| Appeal | Common Techniques | Examples and Rhetorical Effect |
|---|---|---|
| **Pathos – Appeal to Emotion** | Allusions<br>Anecdote<br>Connotations<br>Examples<br>Figurative language<br>Imagery<br>Repetition<br>Sensory details | |
| **Logos – Appeal to Logic** | Allusions<br>Analogies<br>Anecdote<br>Charts<br>Examples<br>Expert sources<br>Facts<br>Graphs<br>Personal testimony<br>Repetition<br>Research<br>Statistics<br>Syntax | |

*Ideas in Argument*, 1e

| | | |
|---|---|---|
| **Ethos – Appeal to Credibility** | Concession<br>Facts<br>Personal testimony<br>Refutation<br>Statistics<br>Sincerity<br>Use of credible and reliable sources<br>Writer's authority and experience | |

**Analyzing Rhetorical Appeals (p. 90)**

As you read the following speech, use the graphic organizer to note the types of appeals Kamala Harris employs to engage her audience.

| Analyzing Rhetorical Appeals | | |
|---|---|---|
| **Appeal** | **Common Techniques** | **Examples and Their Rhetorical Effect** |
| **Pathos – Emotion** | Allusions<br>Anecdote<br>Connotations<br>Examples<br>Figurative language<br>Imagery<br>Repetition<br>Sensory details | |
| **Logos – Logic** | Allusions<br>Analogies<br>Anecdote<br>Charts<br>Examples<br>Expert sources<br>Facts<br>Graphs<br>Statistics<br>Personal testimony<br>Repetition<br>Research<br>Syntax | |
| **Ethos – Credibility** | Concession<br>Facts<br>Personal testimony<br>Refutation<br>Statistics<br>Sincerity<br>Use of credible and reliable sources<br>Writer's authority and experience | |

## Selecting Evidence for an Audience (p. 95)

Think about the same claim you might make to two different audiences. Then, think about the two different audiences. Make a list of the information you could use as evidence. Considering the two different audiences, identify which evidence would be appropriate for each of them.

<table>
<tr><td colspan="2">Claim:</td></tr>
<tr><td>Audience A:</td><td>Audience B:</td></tr>
<tr><td>Evidence:</td><td>Evidence:</td></tr>
</table>

**Connecting Evidence and Audience (p. 96)**

As you read Rushin's argument, make note of the evidence he uses to support his reasons and claim. Considering his audience, how might the evidence appeal to that audience?

| Connecting Evidence to an Audience | | |
|---|---|---|
| **Reason** | **Evidence** | **Effect (Appeal) to an Audience** |
| | | |
| | | |
| | | |
| | | |
| | | |
| | | |
| | | |
| | | |
| | | |

**Establishing a Line of Reasoning (p. 101)**

Think about your message or claim from the previous workshop. What reasons would you use to justify your claim for that audience? How would you organize your argument? With induction or deduction? Why did you make that choice?

| **Audience** | |
|---|---|
| **Claim** | |
| **Line of Reasoning** | |
| **Organization and Rationale** | |

**Analyzing Organization (p. 102)**

As you read her argument, identify the reasons Namgyal uses to persuade her audience. Then consider whether she uses inductive or deductive organization to engage her audience and call them to action. Why do you think she chose this logic?

| **Analyzing Organization** | |
|---|---|
| **Audience** | |
| **Claim** | |
| **Line of Reasoning** | |
| **Organization and Rationale** | |

**Syntax for Effect (p. 107)**

Think about the audience you identified in the previous workshop. Which syntactical moves (e.g., parallel structure, rhetorical questions, repetition, juxtaposition) would you use in an argument to convince that audience?

| **Audience** | |
|---|---|
| **Claim** | |
| **Syntactical Move and Example** | |
| **Syntactical Move and Example** | |
| **Syntactical Move and Example** | |

## Analyzing Syntax (p. 108)

In this informative and impassioned televised address, George W. Bush employed strategic syntactical choices to engage the American people toward a unified call to action. You may use the following graphic organizer as you read and find examples of the following syntactical techniques and consider the effect they had on President Bush's message and on his audience as you answer the questions after the text.

| Analyzing Syntax | | |
|---|---|---|
| **Rhetorical Devices** | **Definition** | **Examples and Effect** |
| Repetition | Repeating or recurrence of a word, phrase, sentence, or other element | |
| Juxtaposition | Contrasting ideas, scenes, settings, images, or other elements | |
| Parallel Structure | Repeating words or phrases in the same grammatical structure | |
| Rhetorical Question | Posing a question that is expected to be considered but not answered literally | |
| Antithesis | Contrasting ideas in parallel grammatical structure | |
| Fragment | Expressing a broken thought or only part of a sentence intentionally | |
| Simple Sentence | Expressing a complete thought consisting of a subject and verb | |

**Selecting Relevant Evidence (p. 143)**

1. Develop a thesis with a call to action about your topic.
2. Brainstorm evidence to support your thesis.

| **Thesis with a Call to Action** | | |
|---|---|---|
| **Possible Evidence** | | |
| **Facts, Statistics, Expert Opinions, Experiments** | **Details, Illustrations, Analogies** | **Personal Experiences or Observations** |
| | | |

**Appealing to an Audience (p. 144)**

Think about your topic and answer the following questions:
- Who is my audience?
- What do I want my audience to do or stop doing? What is my call to action?
- What do they already know and believe about my topic?
- Will the audience be moved more by logic, emotion, or a combination of both?
- How can I connect to my audience or gain their trust?

| Appeal to Logic | Appeal to Emotion | Establishing Credibility |
|---|---|---|
| | | |

**Developing a Line of Reasoning (p. 146)**

List your reasons in support of your claim for your topic and brainstorm the type of evidence that would serve to support your argument.

| Reasons | Evidence to Support Your Reasons |
| --- | --- |
| | |
| | |
| | |

**Developing a Line of Reasoning (p. 147)**

After analyzing your audience, choose either inductive or deductive reasoning to present your claims and evidence. Begin your argument by describing the problem you wish to solve and either stating your claim or posing a question.
(Note: You will learn how to write full introductions and conclusions in later units.)
Choose one of the following methods.

| **Induction** | **Deduction** |
|---|---|
| Describe the problem and then pose a question.<br><br>In the conclusion, present a thesis that answers the question and your call to action. | Describe the problem and present your thesis.<br><br>In the conclusion, explain the significance of the idea and end with your final call to action. |

- Write two or more body paragraphs presenting your reasons and supported with evidence that appeals to your audience.
- Incorporate an explanation and discussion of the evidence.

**Revising and Editing a Persuasive Argument (p. 149)**

| Peer Revision Checklist: Revising and Editing a Persuasive Argument | | |
|---|---|---|
| **Questions to Consider** | **Unit 1 Focus Skills** | **Comment on the Effectiveness and/or Make a Suggestion** |
| Does the claim in the introduction or conclusion establish the writer's point of view on the topic and conclude with a call to action? | *Persuasion* | |
| Is the evidence and commentary arranged in an appropriate manner for the audience? | *Inductive or deductive arrangement* | |
| Has the writer related to, connected with, or appealed to his or her audience? Are these choices effective for the specific audience? | *Logos, ethos, pathos* | |
| Has the writer crafted the piece of persuasion with effective and appropriate rhetorical strategies? | *Antithesis, rhetorical question, repetition, parallelism, juxtaposition* | |
| Is the writing free of errors in spelling, punctuation, capitalization, and other writing conventions? | *Punctuating syntactical features* | |

**Creating Emphasis through Syntax (p. 149)**

- Finish composing your argument.
- Read through the draft of your argument to begin the revision process.
- Incorporate syntactical moves in ways that engage your audience and emphasize your points.

# UNIT 3
# Understanding Context

*Ideas in Argument, 1e*

**Activity Handout: Describing Rhetorical Context (p. 164)**

Identify a rhetorical context that you've been part of and then think about how the historical, cultural, and social values of the time, place, and occasion affected the audience and message.

| Historical, cultural, and social values of the TIME | Historical, cultural, and social values of the PLACE | Historical, cultural, and social values of the OCCASION |
|---|---|---|
| | | |

**Graphic Organizer: Analyzing Context (p. 165)**

Think about the writer, context, and audience before you read the following speech. Predict what you think this writer would say given his audience and context. As you read the speech, identify the writer's major message or thesis. Then explain why the writer would deliver this message to this particular audience in this particular context.

| **Analyzing Rhetorical Context** | | |
|---|---|---|
| Writer | Context<br>-Time<br>-Place<br>-Occasion | Audience |
| Message: | | |
| Explain the significance of the writer's message for this particular audience in this particular context. | | |

**Activity Handout: Identifying Evidence (p. 175)**

Imagine you would like to argue that juniors and seniors at your high school should be allowed to leave campus for lunch. In the chart, identify several sources of evidence you would use to convince two distinct audiences of your perspective: school administrators and parents or guardians of students, respectively. What evidence would likely convince the first audience? How might this choice of evidence be different for the second audience?

| | **Sources of Evidence** | **Type of Evidence** |
|---|---|---|
| Parents or guardians | | |
| School administrators | | |

**Graphic Organizer: Analyzing Sources of Evidence (p. 176)**

As you read the following article, identify the various sources that Stevenson uses. What type of evidence does each source provide? Note how Stevenson introduces each source. How does the way Stevenson introduces the evidence indicate how that evidence relates to other sources of evidence, as well as to Stevenson's message?

| **Analyzing Sources and the Function of Evidence** | | |
|---|---|---|
| Source of Evidence | Type of Evidence | Function of Evidence<br>• How is this evidence introduced?<br>• How does this evidence relate to other pieces of evidence and the overall argument? |
| | | |
| | | |

**Activity Handout: Describing a Line of Reasoning (p. 184)**

Think about a process you've learned about in another class, such as how a bill becomes a law, the stages of mitosis, the steps in the writing process. Identify the steps, stages, or phases of that process. Then briefly state their importance to the overall outcome of the process.

| Step, Stage, or Phase (in Order) | Relationship to Outcome |
|---|---|
| | |
| | |
| | |
| | |
| | |

**Graphic Organizer: Analyzing a Line of Reasoning (p. 185)**

As you read, identify the steps in this process argument that make up the writer's line of reasoning. Identify two specific details within each step and then explain how those details further Goode's claim (both idea and perspective).

| Analyzing Process Arguments | | |
|---|---|---|
| **Message/Thesis:** | | |
| **Step** | **Details** | **Significance to the Writer's Claim (Idea and Perspective)** |
| | | |
| | | |

**Activity Handout: Analyzing Transitions (p. 190)**

Find the lyrics to one of your favorite songs. Identify the transitions used within the song. Explain how the songwriter uses these transitions to convey important relationships and ideas.

| | **Transitions Used** | **Relationship between Ideas, Reasons, or Evidence** |
|---|---|---|
| **Transitions between paragraphs** | | |
| **Transitions introducing sources** | | |
| **Transitions between pieces of evidence** | | |

**Graphic Organizer: Analyzing Transitions (p. 191)**

Identify the transitions the writer uses. Explain the relationship each transition indicates and how that evidence helps to achieve the writer's purpose.

| Analyzing the Effect of Transitions | | |
|---|---|---|
| | **Transitions Used** | **Relationship between Ideas, Reasons, or Evidence** |
| **Transitions between paragraphs** | | |
| **Transitions introducing sources** | | |
| **Transitions between pieces of evidence** | | |

**Activity Handout: Establishing Context (p. 224)**

Think about the subject of your process analysis. Then complete a table like the one above as you reflect on both the context and the ideas associated with your process analysis. For this workshop, we will use “how to organize a closet” as a model.

| **Audience** | **Potential Unifying Ideas** |
| --- | --- |
| | |

**Activity Handout: Establishing a Purpose (p. 225)**

Write a thesis statement for your subject related to your unifying idea and list the major steps or phases of the process.

| Thesis (Subject + Idea) | Steps, Stages, or Phases |
|---|---|
| | |
| | |
| | |

**Activity Handout: Explaining Relevance (p. 227)**

Generate a list of important details for completing each step of the process. Arrange these details in chronological order to support the subject of the paragraph. If you need to include photographs, images, or other graphics, refer to them in your text. You may continue brainstorming on your graphic organizer.
Use the following graphic organizer to arrange your details.

| Thesis (Subject + Idea) | Steps, Stages, or Phases | Details and Explanation |
|---|---|---|
| | | |
| | | |
| | | |

**Graphic Organizer: Revising and Editing a Process Argument (p. 229)**

| Peer Revision Checklist: Revising and Editing a Process Argument | | |
|---|---|---|
| **Questions to Consider** | **Unit 3 Focus Skills** | **Comment on the Effectiveness and/or Make a Suggestion** |
| Does the claim in the introduction or conclusion connect the process to an idea? | *Process analysis/how-to essay* | |
| Are the evidence and commentary divided into phases and arranged in chronological order for the audience? | *Chronological line of reasoning* | |
| Has the writer accounted for the audience's prior knowledge? Did the writer connect the process to a purpose or benefit? | *Audience/purpose* | |
| Has the writer crafted the process essay with clear and specific details connected with transitions that clarify the process? | *Transitions for time or order* | |
| Is the writing free of errors in spelling, punctuation, capitalization, and other writing conventions? | *Punctuating syntactical features* | |

# UNIT 4
# Analyzing Purpose

**Activity Handout: Connecting Purpose and Audience (p. 251)**

Identify an issue or subject that is important to you, such as a hobby, interest, or social issue. What do you want to say about the subject or issue? That will be your message. Next, identify an audience that you could address about that subject. Then, identify one or more purposes that you have for your message. What rhetorical choices could best convey your idea and achieve your purpose given that specific audience? Why choose these strategies?

| **Subject:** | |
|---|---|
| **Message/Idea:** | |
| **Audience:** | |
| **Purpose A** | **Purpose B** |
| | |
| **Rhetorical Choices to Achieve Purpose with That Audience** | **Rhetorical Choices to Achieve Purpose with That Audience** |
| | |

**Graphic Organizer: Describing Purposes (p. 252)**

In the following editorial, Wang considers the AP® U.S. History curriculum. As you read, think about his multiple purposes, as well as the different audiences that he is trying to reach. Consider one of the specific audiences. Then, identify at least two purposes that Wang hoped to achieve with that audience. How does he want to change this audience's views or behaviors? What rhetorical choices does Wang draw upon to achieve his overall purpose with different audiences? Use the graphic organizer that follows to record your observations.

| **Analyzing Multiple Purposes of an Argument** | |
|---|---|
| **Subject:** | |
| **Message/Idea:** | |
| **Audience:** | |
| **Purpose A** | **Purpose B** |
| | |
| **Rhetorical Choices to Achieve Purpose with Audience** | **Rhetorical Choices to Achieve Purpose with Audience** |
| | |

**Activity Handout: Selecting Evidence Strategically (p. 256)**

Choose a policy issue that the local school board or education authority might consider, such as school uniforms, year-round school, or the elimination of standardized testing. Next, identify one additional audience, such as students, parents, educators, or lawmakers, with whom you can address the issue. After you've identified your claim (idea and perspective), select one of the potential audiences and respond to the following prompts:

• List the reasons that you would use to justify your claim with that specific audience.
• Identify the evidence that you would use to support each reason and appeal to that specific audience.
• Explain why you believe that evidence would be most effective for that specific audience.

| **Audience:** | | |
|---|---|---|
| **Claim:** | | |
| **Reasons** | **Evidence** | **Function of Evidence** |
| | | |
| | | |
| | | |
| | | |

**Graphic Organizer: Explaining the Function of Evidence (p. 257)**

In the following article, the writers examine the importance of activism to Generation Z. Identify the intended audience and the writers' claim. Next, identify the reasons used to justify the claim. Then, describe the evidence and explain how it functions to appeal to the intended audience.

| Explaining the Function of Evidence | | |
|---|---|---|
| **Audience:** | | |
| **Claim:** | | |
| **Reasons** | **Evidence** | **Function of Evidence** |
| | | |
| | | |
| | | |
| | | |

## Activity Handout: Creating a Definition Argument (p. 264)

Think of a term or concept that could be presented through definition. You might consider a concept such as the following:

- A good education
- A literary or artistic movement, such as Romanticism
- A type of government, such as democracy or autocracy
- A principle such as justice, friendship, or greed

In the following table, note the traits, attributes, characteristics, or qualities of the term that would serve as reasons to justify your definition of it. Then, identify some examples, illustrations, analogies, or contrasts that you might use to support each reason.

| **Term or Concept to Be Defined:** | |
|---|---|
| **Trait, Attribute, Feature, Characteristic, or Quality** | **Example, Illustration, Analogy, or Contrast** |
| | |
| | |
| | |

## Graphic Organizer: Analyzing Definition Arguments (p. 265)

In this essay, Crèvecoeur asks and answers the question, "What is an American?" Use the following graphic organizer to note how Crèvecoeur defines an "American" by presenting characteristics and traits, as well as examples and illustrations.

| Analyzing Definition Arguments | |
|---|---|
| **Trait, Attribute, Feature, Characteristic, or Quality** | **Example, Illustration, Analogy, or Contrast** |
| | |
| | |
| | |
| | |

**Activity Handout: Explaining the Effects of Ambiguity (p. 270)**

Consider each of the following statements, which illustrate different types of ambiguities. Explain what is ambiguous and how that affects meaning.

| Types of Ambiguity | Effect on Meaning |
|---|---|
| **Pronoun References**<br>At lunch, one of your friends says the following:<br><br>"They said that all assignments were going to be pass/fail in the future." | |
| **Misplaced Modifiers**<br>The following announcement was heard on the school intercom:<br><br>"Hitting the winning run in the game last night, the coach awarded Johnny most valuable player." | |
| **Inflated Diction**<br>The following appeared in a student-written article for the online school paper:<br><br>"The third-year athlete allowed the team to be victorious by causing his opponent to relinquish the ball in the penultimate quarter of the athletic contest." | |

**Graphic Organizer: Explaining the Effects of Ambiguity (p. 271)**

Use the following graphic organizer to identify any examples of ambiguity in Harmon's article. What is the effect of this ambiguity? Keep in mind that writers may intentionally and strategically create ambiguity.

| **Explaining the Effects of Ambiguity** | |
|---|---|
| **Types of Ambiguity and Example** | **Effect on Meaning** |
| **Pronoun References:** | |
| **Misplaced Modifiers:** | |
| **Inflated Diction:** | |

**Activity Handout: Connecting Audience and Purpose (p. 308)**

1. Consider the context for your extended definition.
2. Choose an engaging hook to begin your argument.
3. Write an introduction for your definition argument.

| What is the concept that you are defining? | |
|---|---|
| Who is your audience? | |
| What is your purpose(s)? | |
| How will you orient, engage, or focus the audience? | |

**Activity Handout: Explaining Significance (p. 309)**

1. Create a word web with as many attributes and characteristics as you can generate for your concept. You might consider synonyms, antonyms, and word origins to help you brainstorm. Next, sort the list by common ideas.

2. Circle three or four of the best attributes to use as topic sentences for your body paragraphs. Note: You may also organize part of your discussion around what the concept is not.

3. Explain the significance of each reason in relation to your unifying idea.

| **Concept to Be Defined:** | | |
|---|---|---|
| **Unifying Idea and Perspective:** | | |
| **Characteristic 1** | **Characteristic 2** | **Characteristic 3** |
| Significance to Unifying Idea | Significance to Unifying Idea | Significance to Unifying Idea |

**Graphic Organizer: Revising and Editing a Definition Argument (p. 314)**

| **Peer Revision Checklist: Revising and Editing a Definition Argument** | | |
|---|---|---|
| **Revising and Editing Checklist** | **Unit 4 Focus Skills** | **Comment on the Effectiveness and/or Make a Suggestion** |
| Does the claim in the introduction or conclusion connect the concept to a perspective? | Definition argument | |
| Is the evidence and commentary organized by attributes or qualities of the concept? | Line of reasoning | |
| Has the writer developed the definition with effective and appropriate evidence? | Analogies and comparisons | |
| Has the writer explained the evidence and connected the concept to the perspective? Are these choices effective for the specific audience and purpose? | Developing commentary | |
| Is the writing clear and specific? Is the diction precise? Is the writing free of error in pronoun references and misplaced and dangling modifiers? | Avoiding ambiguity | |
| Is the writing free of errors in spelling, usage, punctuation, capitalization, and agreement? | Writing conventions | |

**Graphic Organizer: Supporting Your Thesis (p. 319)**

| **Thesis (Message + Choices)** | | |
|---|---|---|
| **Developing a Body Paragraph** | **Reasons** | |
| **IDENTIFY**<br>Topic Sentences: Identify the reason (a strategy) and the devices the writer uses to develop that strategy | **Strategy:**<br><br>**Devices:** | **Strategy:**<br><br>**Devices:** |
| **EVIDENCE**<br>Textual Evidence: Exemplify the message and identify author choices | **Text evidence:** | **Text evidence:** |
| **LINK**<br>Provide commentary that connects the choices to the message (idea) by explaining the significance in relation to the claim (idea + perspective) | **Commentary:** | **Commentary:** |

# UNIT 5
# Creating Coherence

**Activity Handout: Describing Exigence (p. 336)**

Consider the following scenarios and connect your exigence with purpose, audience, and message.

| | **Scenario A**<br><br>An issue or situation that angered or provoked you | **Scenario B**<br><br>A situation or event where you felt gratitude or inspiration |
|---|---|---|
| What is the exigence? | | |
| What is the issue? | | |
| What is your position, perspective, and message? | | |
| What is your goal? | | |
| Who will you communicate with to achieve your goal? | | |
| How will you communicate your message? | | |

**Graphic Organizer: Describing Exigence (p. 337)**

Before you read P!NK's speech, identify her exigence by considering the following questions. As you read, consider how her exigence is related to her overall purpose.

| Determining the Writer's Exigence | |
|---|---|
| What is the context of the speech? | |
| What is the writer's role in this context? | |
| What is the writer's relationship to the audience? | |
| What is the writer's relationship to the issue? | |
| **The Writer's Purpose** | |
| | |

**Activity Handout: Arranging Evidence for Coherence (p. 340)**

Consider the following purposes and audiences as a writer. What method would you use to arrange your reasons and evidence? Why?

| Purpose and Audience | Method of Arrangement | Rationale |
|---|---|---|
| You're telling an entertaining story to your best friend. | | |
| You're writing a proposal to gain permission from the principal to start a new school club. | | |
| You're creating a podcast episode on the effects of climate change for your local community. | | |
| You're explaining the effects of a health issue in an academic paper for your health teacher. | | |
| You're describing a place that you visited on a trip. | | |

**Graphic Organizer: Analyzing Evidence (p. 342)**

In the following essay, Watson uses transitions to move from point to point. Use the following graphic organizer to identify the transitions Watson uses and describe the relationships these transitions convey.

| Analyzing Arrangement | | |
|---|---|---|
| **Transition and Location** | **Organization and Arrangement** | **Function and Effect** |
| | | |
| | | |
| | | |
| | | |

**Activity Handout: Organizing by Cause and Effect (p. 348)**

1. Examining Causes. Think of an event (social, political, natural) that has happened within the last month. What are the likely causes of that event?

| Causes | | Effect |
|---|---|---|
| | | |
| | | |
| | **Leads to** | |
| | | |

2. Examining Effects. Now, think of something that is happening right now or within the last two days. What are the likely effects of that event or issue?

| Event/Issue | | Effects |
|---|---|---|
| | | |
| | **Precipitated** | |
| | | |
| | | |

**Graphic Organizer: Analyzing Causal Arguments (p. 349)**

As you read “How Sesame Street Started a Musical Revolution,” identify the causal factors that Ryzik describes. How do they serve as her line of reasoning?

<table>
<tr><th colspan="2">Analyzing Causal Arguments</th></tr>
<tr><th>Causes</th><th>Effect</th></tr>
<tr><td></td><td rowspan="5"></td></tr>
<tr><td></td></tr>
<tr><td></td></tr>
<tr><td></td></tr>
<tr><td></td></tr>
</table>

**Activity Handout: Analyzing Syntax (p. 359)**

Consider the following sentence pairs. Each pair presents the same information; however, the writer is evaluating which syntax would be more effective. How do changes in syntax change the meaning of the sentences? Explain the differences in each pair.

| **Subordination**<br>*While I was cooking dinner last night, I found out that I won a full scholarship.*<br>*While I found out that I won a full scholarship last night, I was cooking dinner.* |
|---|
| |
| **Coordination**<br>*He is afraid of heights. He enjoyed skydiving with his friends.*<br>*He is afraid of heights, but he enjoyed skydiving with his friends.* |
| |

## Graphic Organizer: Analyzing Syntax (p. 360)

As you read Narain Dubey's article, identify examples of his syntactical choices. For each example, describe its function within the argument.

| Analyzing the Effects of Syntax | | |
|---|---|---|
| **Questions to Consider for Syntactical Choices**<br><br>• Why has the writer arranged the sentences in this order?<br>• Does the writer use simple sentences to present the main idea?<br>• How do the main ideas within individual sentences contribute to the writer's claim?<br>• Why has the writer presented the main idea first (or last) in a specific sentence?<br>• What is the relationship between the ideas within a particular sentence?<br>• How do the relationships presented within sentences reinforce the writer's overall argument? | | |
| **Syntactical Strategy** | **Effect/Function** | **Example** |
| Coordination | indicates equal ideas<br><br>shows balance of ideas | |
| Subordination | indicates inequality of ideas<br><br>emphasizes one idea over another<br><br>builds suspense<br><br>provides causal information/ details | |
| Simple Sentence | emphasizes the main idea | |
| Rhetorical Question | asks the reader to pause and reflect | |
| Intentional Fragment | highlights an idea | |

**Activity Handout: Writing an Introduction (p. 406)**

1. Make a list of possible subjects for your causal argument. Consider both cause-driven subjects and effect-driven subjects.

2. Choose either a cause-driven or effect-driven subject. Then record details related to your exigence in a chart. Consider how you might use some of these details in your argument.

| **Exigence** | **Issue One: Focus on Causes**<br>What causes result from a single effect? |
|---|---|
| Describe the subject and why it is important to you. | |
| Describe your perspective and message for your audience. | |
| Explain your goal for sharing your perspective. | |
| List details and possible evidence related to your subject. | |

**Activity Handout: Unifying an Argument (p. 409)**

1. Review your brainstorming notes on subject and exigence.
2. Develop your thesis statement by combining the unifying idea and your perspective.
3. Review the details and possible evidence for your subject.
4. Compose topic sentences communicating the causes or effects of your subject.

Carefully consider the order in which you will present these topic sentences.

5. Plan a conclusion that unifies your message and relates back to the central cause or effect in your thesis.

| | |
|---|---|
| Thesis with claim<br>(idea + perspective) | |
| Cause or effect 1<br>Topic sentence | |
| Cause or effect 2<br>Topic sentence | |
| Cause or effect 3<br>Topic sentence | |
| Effect or cause<br>Conclusion | |

**Activity Handout: Connecting Relevant Evidence (p. 411)**

1. Revisit your thesis statement and your topic sentences. Make any necessary changes to ensure that you are developing a unified argument.

2. Review the order of your topic sentences and explain the order of your line of reasoning.

3. Generate specific evidence to exemplify your topic sentences and convey your message.

4. Carefully arrange your evidence within the body paragraphs. More generally, arrange your evidence in a logical order within each paragraph to demonstrate the connections and emerging relationships between causes and effects.

| **Thesis with Claim (Idea + Perspective)** | | |
|---|---|---|
| **Topic Sentence Reason 1 (Cause or Effect)** | **Topic Sentence Reason 2 (Cause or Effect)** | **Topic Sentence Reason 3 (Cause or Effect)** |
| Supporting Evidence | Supporting Evidence | Supporting Evidence |
| Supporting Evidence | Supporting Evidence | Supporting Evidence |

**Graphic Organizer: Revising and Editing a Causal Argument (p. 415)**

| Peer Revision Checklist: Revising and Editing a Causal Argument | | |
|---|---|---|
| **Revising and Editing Checklist** | **Unit 5 Focus Skills** | **Comment on the Effectiveness and/or Make a Suggestion** |
| Does the claim in the introduction or conclusion connect the subject to an idea and perspective? | *Causal argument* | |
| Are the evidence and commentary organized by causes, effects, or the cause-effect relationship of the concept? | *Line of reasoning* | |
| Has the writer developed the argument with relevant and sufficient evidence that logically links to the line of reasoning? | *Unity and coherence* | |
| Has the writer explained the evidence and connected the causes or effects to the perspective?<br><br>Are these choices effective for the specific audience and purpose? | *Developing commentary* | |
| Is the writing clear and specific?<br><br>Does the writer use syntax (subordination and coordination) to link ideas logically and amplify the relationship between causes, effects, and the issue? | *Syntax for emphasis* | |
| Is the writing free of errors in spelling, usage, punctuation, capitalization, and agreement? | *Writing conventions* | |

# UNIT 6

## Establishing and Evaluating Credibility

**Activity Handout: Establishing Ethos (p. 432)**

Consider something that you know or understand well (e.g., a hobby, an interest, a personal experience) and identify an unknown audience that you'd share that knowledge with. Briefly explain how you could establish your ethos.

| **Subject:** | | |
|---|---|---|
| **Audience:** | | |
| **Ways You Can Establish Ethos** | **Relevant Aspects of Your Identity** | **How would you establish your ethos?**<br><br>**What details would you present to establish credibility?** |
| • Credibility<br>• Authority<br>• Trustworthiness<br>• Relationship to Audience | • Age<br>• Gender<br>• Location<br>• Religious or cultural values<br>• Position or title<br>• Work experience<br>• Racial or ethnic background<br>• Socioeconomic class<br>• Personal experience<br>• Level of education<br>• Occupation or skill | |

**Graphic Organizer: Analyzing a Writer's Ethos (p. 433)**

As you read the following article, identify details from the argument that contribute to the writer's credibility.

| Analyzing a Writer's Ethos | | |
|---|---|---|
| **Ways a Writer Can Establish Ethos** | **Relevant Aspects of the Writer's Identity** | **Details in the Text** |
| • Credibility<br>• Authority<br>• Trustworthiness<br>• Relationship with the audience | • Age<br>• Gender<br>• Location<br>• Religious or cultural values<br>• Position or title<br>• Work experience<br>• Racial or ethnic background<br>• Socioeconomic class<br>• Personal experience<br>• Level of education<br>• Occupation or skill | |

**Activity Handout: Evaluating a Source's Perspective (p. 440)**

Think of a current issue or subject that interests you. Then, identify four sources that might provide information about this issue. Consider what you know about each source, identifying potential biases that would affect the source's credibility and reliability. Finally, reflect on how receiving information from only those sources would influence your own perspective on the subject.

| **Subject/Issue:** | | | |
|---|---|---|---|
| **Source** | **Position and Information about the Subject Provided by the Source** | **Potential Biases** | **How That Source Affects Your Perspective** |
| | | | |
| | | | |
| | | | |
| | | | |

**Graphic Organizer: Explaining the Function of Evidence (p. 441)**

As you read Barber's argument, identify his supporting evidence for each line of reasoning. Next, consider how the evidence may function in appealing to his audience. Then, explain how the inclusion and arrangement of this evidence within the argument further the claim in his thesis.

| Analyzing the Function of Evidence | | |
|---|---|---|
| **Writer's Thesis (Identify Perspective and Unifying Idea):** | | |
| **Evidence** | **Function of Evidence** | **How does the writer's strategic inclusion and arrangement of this evidence affect the message?** |
| | | |
| | | |
| | | |
| | | |
| | | |

**Activity Handout: Organizing by Classification or Division (p. 447)**

Choose a concept (e.g., high school classes, musical artists, phone apps, teachers) that you can break down into two or more categories. Next, identify the types or kinds and explain their significance. Then, describe the attributes of each type and give specific examples.

| **Concept:** | | | |
|---|---|---|---|
| **Type, Category, or Part** | **Significance** | **Traits/Attributes** | **Examples** |
| | | | |
| | | | |
| | | | |
| | | | |
| | | | |
| | | | |

## Graphic Organizer: Analyzing Arguments of Classification/Division (p. 448)

As you read Kaling's argument, identify her categories of classification, as well as the traits or attributes of each category. Cite specific textual evidence to illustrate each of the attributes and give examples. What is the significance of each category of classification (or division) for her overall message? What values does her classification method suggest?

| Analyzing Classification and Definition Arguments | | | |
|---|---|---|---|
| **Concept or Value of Classification Method:** | | | |
| **Thesis:** | | | |
| **Type, Category, or Part** | **Significance of the Type of Classification or Division** | **Traits/Attributes** | **Examples** |
| | | | |
| | | | |
| | | | |
| | | | |
| | | | |
| | | | |

**Activity Handout: Choosing Precise Diction (p. 454)**

Tone can be tricky to detect, even in our daily text-message conversations. Think about your own experience sending and receiving emojis. What tones do they convey? For each of the following examples, provide words that could accurately describe the tone of that emoji depending on the context.

| Emoji | Context | Potential Tones |
|---|---|---|
|  | | |
|  | | |
|  | | |
|  | | |
| You choose another emoji | | |

**Graphic Organizer: Describing Tone (p. 455)**

As you read "A Hunger for Books," use the following organizer to identify a shift in the writer's tone. Next, record the diction used before the shift and the diction used after the shift. Examine each group of words. Then, choose one adjective that describes the tone before the shift and one adjective that describes the tone after the shift.

<table>
<tr><th colspan="2">Identifying Shifts in Tone</th></tr>
<tr><td colspan="2">Cite text that indicates a shift in tone:</td></tr>
<tr><td>Diction before the shift:</td><td>Diction after the shift:</td></tr>
<tr><td>Shifts from:</td><td>Shifts to:</td></tr>
</table>

**Activity Handout: Synthesizing Evidence (p. 491)**

1. List as many details as you can generate about your subject or concept.
2. Consider different sources of evidence and determine the function and purpose of each.

| Type of Evidence from Sources | Evidence | Function and Purpose |
|---|---|---|
| Personal experience | | |
| Information from others | | |
| Statistics and data | | |
| Research | | |
| Case studies | | |
| Interviews, surveys, and real-life examples | | |

**Activity Handout: Arranging Reasons and Evidence (p. 494)**

1. Review the categories or component parts that you have identified in your line of reasoning, along with the identifying attributes and evidence that you have generated to illustrate those attributes.
2. Arrange your evidence strategically (spatial, chronological, level of importance, or level of specificity). Keep your audience and purpose in mind as you make these choices.
3. Review your original thesis or claim and make any necessary revisions based on your line of reasoning and evidence.
4. Begin writing by introducing your subject, providing context, and identifying the categories or principle of division that you will use to develop your argument.

<table>
<tr><th colspan="4">Concept</th></tr>
<tr><th>Types/Parts</th><th>Significance</th><th>Traits/Attributes</th><th>Examples</th></tr>
<tr><td rowspan="2"></td><td rowspan="2"></td><td></td><td></td></tr>
<tr><td></td><td></td></tr>
<tr><td rowspan="2"></td><td rowspan="2"></td><td></td><td></td></tr>
<tr><td></td><td></td></tr>
<tr><td rowspan="2"></td><td rowspan="2"></td><td></td><td></td></tr>
<tr><td></td><td></td></tr>
</table>

**Activity Handout: Using Precise Diction (p. 496)**

In the space below, identify the attitude you wish to convey about your subject. In the middle column, write a few sentences about your subject. Then, in the right-hand column, rewrite the sentences using precise diction and syntax that communicate that attitude through tone.

| Attitude Toward Subject | Initial Sentences | Revised Sentences |
|---|---|---|
| | | |
| | | |
| | | |

## Graphic Organizer: Revising and Editing a Classification/Division Argument (p. 497)

| **Peer Revision Checklist: Revising and Editing a Classification/Division Argument** | | |
|---|---|---|
| **Revising and Editing Checklist** | **Unit 6 Focus Skills** | **Comment on the Effectiveness and/or Make a Suggestion** |
| Does the claim in the introduction or conclusion connect the subject to a perspective? | *Classification/division argument* | |
| Is the evidence and commentary organized by the different types or parts of the subject? Does the writer organize the argument inductively? Deductively? | *Line of reasoning* | |
| Has the writer developed the argument with a variety of effective and appropriate evidence? | *Multiple sources* | |
| Has the writer explained the evidence and connected the subject to his or her perspective? Are these choices effective for the specific audience and purpose? | *Developing commentary* | |
| Is the writing clear and specific? Does the word choice convey the writer's attitude toward the subject? | *Conveying a tone* | |
| Is the writing free of errors in spelling, usage, punctuation, capitalization, and agreement? | *Writing conventions* | |

# UNIT 7
# Comparing Perspectives

**Activity Handout: Analyzing the Rhetorical Situation (p. 522)**

Think of a familiar rhetorical situation that you've been a part of, such as writing a letter, making a phone call, persuading friends, or delivering a speech. Use the following organizer to illustrate the relationships among context, writer, and audience.

<table>
<tr><td colspan="2">Rhetorical Situation:</td></tr>
<tr><td colspan="2">Context<br>1. What is the time, place, occasion?<br><br>2. What is going on culturally or socially that affects the writer and audience?</td></tr>
<tr><td>Writer<br><br>• What is your relationship to this audience?<br>• What is your perspective on the subject?<br>• What is your purpose?<br>• What is your relationship to the subject?</td><td>Audience<br><br>• Who is the intended audience?<br>• What are their beliefs, values?<br>• What attitudes and biases might they have toward the subject?</td></tr>
</table>

## Graphic Organizer: Analyzing Relationships within a Rhetorical Situation (p. 523)

As you read Kim's argument, consider when it was written and by whom. Find textual evidence within Kim's introduction and conclusion that provides clues about the context, writer, and audience. Then draw inferences about the relationships between (and among) the writer, audience, and context that influence the writer's rhetorical choices.

| Analyzing Relationships within a Rhetorical Situation | |
|---|---|
| Context | |
| Writer | Audience |

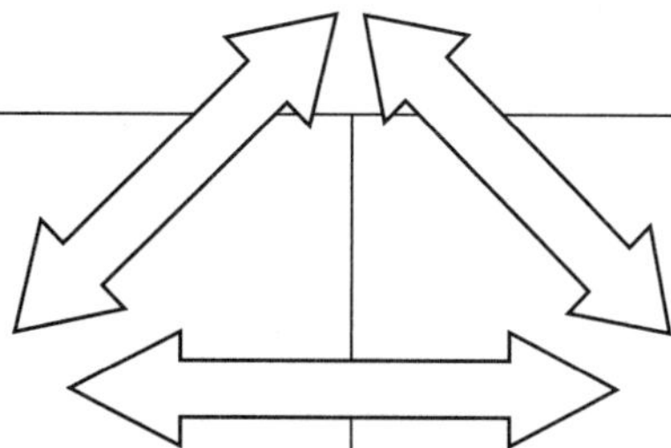

**Activity Handout: Qualifying an Argument (p. 528)**

Pick a subject or issue of current interest in your school or community. Then develop a claim and select evidence to defend it. Next, develop a claim that challenges your initial claim. Finally, use strategies you learned in this workshop to qualify your first claim with a concession to the second one.

| **Subject:** | | |
|---|---|---|
| **Defense of Claim** | **Challenge of Claim** | **Qualification of Claim** |
| | | |

**Graphic Organizer: Analyzing Qualification and Concession (p. 529)**

| Analyzing Qualification and Concession | | |
|---|---|---|
| **Claim and Defense**<br>Identify the writer's primary claim and defense (reasons that justify that claim). | **Qualification**<br>Identify statements and evidence that qualify the writer's claim. | **Concession**<br>Identify statements and evidence that offer the writer's concession to other perspectives |
| | | |

**Activity Handout: Identifying Categories of Comparison (p. 534)**

Choose one of the following activities (or develop a similar one of your own). Then use comparison and contrast to evaluate the two options. To make an effective evaluation, develop the categories of comparison.

- Purchasing a pet
- Choosing a vacation location
- Deciding what to do over spring break
- Selecting a sport to play or activity to join

| **Subject:**<br><br>**Goal/Purpose:** | | |
|---|---|---|
| | **Option 1** | **Option 2** |
| **Category of Comparison A** | | |
| **Category of Comparison B** | | |
| **Category of Comparison C** | | |

## Graphic Organizer: Evaluating through Comparison and Contrast (p. 535)

Britt organizes her argument by comparing each of her subjects. As you read the text, use the following organizer to track Britt's reasons and evidence. Pay particular attention to Britt's categories of comparison. How does she use these categories to make a final evaluation part of her claim?

| Evaluating through Comparison and Contrast Subject by Subject | | |
|---|---|---|
| | **Categories of Comparison** | **Details and Evidence** |
| **Subject A** | First Category of Comparison:<br><br>Second Category of Comparison:<br><br>Third Category of Comparison: | |
| **Subject B** | First Category of Comparison:<br><br>Second Category of Comparison:<br><br>Third Category of Comparison: | |
| **Conclusion** | Recommendation/Evaluation: | |

**Activity Handout: Crafting Syntax for a Purpose (p. 541)**

1. Write ten short, simple sentences that tell a story in chronological order, such as a narrative account of your summer vacation. The sentences should convey your story and include a beginning, a middle, and an end.
2. Then combine the sentences in ways that illustrate different meanings. For example:
   - Identify your main idea and leave it as a stand-alone simple sentence.
   - Combine two of your simple sentences that illustrate equal ideas by using a coordinating conjunction.
   - Identify one sentence that shows a cause-and-effect relationship or that is dependent on another sentence; combine those two sentences using a subordinating conjunction.
   - Examine the remaining sentences and then combine them using coordination or subordination, as you did with the previous sentences.
   - Combine two of the sentences (or add a sentence, if necessary) so that you're using an adjective clause of appositive to further clarify or describe a noun.
   - Include another example of strategic punctuation (e.g., dash, parenthetical expressions, rhetorical question) in a purposeful way.
3. Compare your revision with your original. How did your syntactical choices help create a desired rhetorical effect?

**Graphic Organizer: Analyzing Syntactical Choices (p. 542)**

As you read "The 'Loser Edit' That Awaits Us All," pay close attention to Whitehead's syntactical choices, especially his use of punctuation. Use the following table to identify examples of his intentional syntax. Note: Whitehead may not attempt all of the purposes identified in the chart.

| Analyzing Syntactical Choices | | |
|---|---|---|
| **Rhetorical Function** | **Syntactical and Grammatical Structure** | **Example and Rhetorical Effect** |
| Emphasis | Short, simple sentence ending with a period ( . ) | |
| | Two sentences that express the same idea differently connected with a colon ( : ) | |
| | Sentence that sets off information with a dash ( — ) | |
| Balance | Sentence with two independent clauses connected with a comma ( , ) and a coordinating conjunction | |
| | Sentence with a list of words and phrases in a series separated with commas; a coordinating conjunction is used before the final word or phrase in the series to indicate equality | |
| Relationships | Sentence with a subordinate clause set off with a comma ( , ) | |
| Clarification | Sentence with an adjective clause introduced by a relative pronoun (e.g., who, whose, whom, which, that) to indicate specificity | |

| | | |
|---|---|---|
| Detail or Description | Sentence with an appositive phrase set off with commas ( , ) | |
| Exemplification | Sentence with examples (e.g.,) or a clarification (i.e.,) in parentheses | |
| Connection | Sentence with information or detail placed within parentheses ( ( ) ) | |
| Omission | Sentence with ellipses . . . that indicate omitted information or omitted words in direct quotation | |

**Activity Handout: Introducing and Concluding an Argument (p. 593)**

Begin planning your comparison-contrast argument by considering the following:

- What is my main subject?
- What are the categories of comparison?
- What is the purpose of the comparison?
- What is the context for the comparison?
- Who is the audience?
- What is my unifying idea?
- What is my perspective?

**Graphic Organizer: Unifying an Argument (p. 596)**

Plan your comparison-contrast argument using the following chart:

1. Choose either the subject-by-subject or the category-by-category outline.
2. Record notes for your introduction (including hook, context, and question).
3. Compose topic sentences that convey a perspective (either by subject or category).
4. Record notes for your conclusion (answering your question through evaluation and recommendation).

<table>
<tr><th colspan="4">Organizing Evaluation Arguments: Comparison and Contrast</th></tr>
<tr><th colspan="2">SUBJECT BY SUBJECT</th><th colspan="2">CATEGORY BY CATEGORY</th></tr>
<tr><td colspan="2">Introduction</td><td colspan="2">Introduction</td></tr>
<tr><td>Subject A</td><td>First Category of Comparison<br><br>Second Category of Comparison<br><br>Third Category of Comparison</td><td>First Category of Comparison</td><td>Subject A<br><br>Subject B</td></tr>
<tr><td rowspan="2">Subject B</td><td rowspan="2">First Category of Comparison<br><br>Second Category of Comparison<br><br>Third Category of Comparison</td><td>Second Category of Comparison</td><td>Subject A<br><br>Subject B</td></tr>
<tr><td>Third Category of Comparison</td><td>Subject A<br><br>Subject B</td></tr>
<tr><td colspan="2">Conclusion: Recommendation/Evaluation</td><td colspan="2">Conclusion: Recommendation/Evaluation</td></tr>
</table>

**Graphic Organizer: Revising and Editing a Comparison/Contrast Argument (p. 601)**

| Peer Revision Checklist: Revising and Editing a Comparison/Contrast Argument | | |
|---|---|---|
| **Revising and Editing Checklist** | **Unit 7 Focus Skills** | **Comment on the Effectiveness and/or Make a Suggestion** |
| Does the claim in the introduction or conclusion connect the audience to the writer's unifying idea and perspective? | *Narrative distance* | |
| Are the comparisons, evidence, and commentary organized subject by subject or category by category? Is each subject evaluated using the same categories of comparison? | *Line of reasoning (comparison-contrast)* | |
| Has the writer developed the argument with a variety of relevant and sufficient evidence? Does the writer recognize the inherent complexities of the argument by using qualifying language? | *Qualifying an argument* | |
| Has the writer explained the evidence and connected the subjects and categories of comparison? Are these choices effective for the specific audience and purpose? | *Comparison/contrast argument* | |
| Is the writing clear and specific? Do the syntactical choices contribute to the purpose? | *Strategic syntax and punctuation* | |
| Is the writing free of errors in spelling, usage, punctuation, capitalization, and agreement? | *Writing conventions* | |

# UNIT 8
# Explaining Complexities

**Graphic Organizer: Analyzing Rhetorical Comparisons (p. 621)**

As you read Jacob's article, use the following graphic organizer to record any rhetorical comparisons that she uses. Briefly describe how these examples help Jacob communicate her message to her audience.

| Analyzing Rhetorical Comparisons for an Audience | | |
|---|---|---|
| **Organizational Choice** | **Description** | **Example and Intended Effect on Audience** |
| Analogy | Presents two things as similar based on common attributes and then draws an inference, hypothesis, or conclusion about a similarity that has yet to occur or be observed | |
| Extended Metaphor | • Establishes a comparison that extends throughout the argument between two unlike things<br><br>• Draws attention to the shared characteristics that emphasize a value or idea critical to the writer's claim | |
| Allusion | Refers to history, pop culture, literature, or art that the audience knows as a way of illustrating a similarity | |

**Activity Handout: Identifying Counterarguments (p. 627)**

Take a position on a complex or controversial issue in your school or community. Write a claim that includes your position, a controlling or unifying idea, and your perspective. Then consider other perspectives that might support, complement, question, or contradict your claim. Describe how you would offer refutation, concession, or rebuttal to address those competing positions.

| **Issue:** | | |
|---|---|---|
| **Claim:** (position, idea, and perspective) | | |
| **Refutation** | **Concession** | **Rebuttal** |
| | | |

**Graphic Organizer: Identifying Refutation, Concession, and Rebuttal (p. 628)**

As you read Ivins's editorial, describe how she responds to differing or opposing views through refutation, concession, and rebuttal.

| **Identifying Refutation, Concession, and Rebuttal** | | |
|---|---|---|
| **Rhetorical Move** | **Definition** | **Example and Effect** |
| Refutation | Demonstrates with evidence that all (or a portion) of a claim is invalid | |
| Concession | Accepts all (or a portion) of a competing claim as correct, or correct under different circumstances, or acknowledges the limitations of the writer's own argument | |
| Rebuttal | Offers a contrasting perspective on an argument and its evidence or provides alternative evidence to propose that all (or a portion) of a competing claim is invalid | |

**Activity Handout: Proposing a Solution (p. 632)**

Imagine that a local community is concerned about record low voter turnout among eighteen-year-olds in the most recent election. You have been asked to propose a solution to this problem. Before you consider possible solutions, you must identify the goal or criteria for success. Identify three or four potential goals or criteria. Then identify one that you will use when evaluating possible alternatives and solutions.

| **Issue:** Record low voter turnout of eighteen-year-olds | |
|---|---|
| **Potential Success Criterion** | |
| **Potential Success Criterion** | |
| **Potential Success Criterion** | |
| **Potential Success Criterion** | |
| **Final Selection for Success Criterion:** | |

**Graphic Organizer: Analyzing Evaluation Arguments That Propose a Solution (p. 633)**

As you read the text, consider how Jankowski draws on description, compare and contrast, and persuasion to develop his argument. Use the organizer to record details from the text included in each method of development. Then explain how each method of development and its supporting details contribute to the overall argument.

| Understanding a Problem-Solution Argument | | | |
|---|---|---|---|
| | Method of Development | | |
| | **Description** | **Evaluation through Comparison-Contrast** | **Persuasion** |
| **Details from Text** | | | |
| **Purpose or Function in Argument** | | | |

**Activity Handout: Identifying Contrast and Incongruity (p. 639)**

Choose a contemporary social media meme or an example of satire (e.g., a post on Instagram or Twitter, a sketch from *Saturday Night Live*, or an article from *The Onion*). First, describe the literal or surface meaning of the text or images. Then explain how your chosen example draws on irony, incongruity, understatement, or other satirical elements to mock its subject and entertain its audience.

| **Subject:** | | |
|---|---|---|
| **Literal Description:** | | |
| | Example | Purpose and Commentary |
| **Irony** | | |
| **Sarcasm** | | |
| **Juxtaposition** | | |
| **Pun** | | |
| **Hyperbole** | | |
| **Understatement** | | |

**Graphic Organizer: Analyzing Contrast and Incongruity (p. 640)**

As you read "Trendy Restaurant Menu," notice how Wei uses contrasts and incongruities to convey her message. Use the following organizer to identify specific examples and then explain their purpose within her argument.

| **Subject:** | | |
|---|---|---|
| **Literal Description:** | | |
| | Example | Purpose and Commentary |
| **Irony** | | |
| **Sarcasm** | | |
| **Juxtaposition** | | |
| **Pun** | | |
| **Hyperbole** | | |
| **Understatement** | | |

**Activity Handout: Addressing Complexity (p. 677)**

Begin planning your problem-solution argument by considering the following:

- What problem would I like to solve?
- What are the causes and effects of the problem?
- What are the consequences if the problem goes unsolved?
- Who is my audience?
- What alternative perspectives should be addressed?
- What solution will I recommend to my audience in the conclusion?

**Activity Handout: Justifying a Claim (p. 680)**

As you begin drafting your problem-solution argument, complete the following steps:

1. Review your notes for context, complexity, and audience before crafting your introduction.

2. Write a thesis statement that includes a claim and identifies your goal.

3. Generate possible solutions for your line of reasoning.

<table>
<tr><td colspan="3">Problem</td></tr>
<tr><td colspan="3">Introduction<br>Describe and contextualize the problem:<br><br>Establish Success Criteria:</td></tr>
<tr><td>Option One</td><td>Option Two</td><td>Option Three (optional)</td></tr>
<tr><td colspan="3">Proposed Solution</td></tr>
<tr><td colspan="3">Thesis: (unifying idea + perspective) + a goal or success criterion</td></tr>
</table>

**Activity Handout: Developing a Counterargument (p. 684)**

Using the thesis and line of reasoning (i.e., possible solutions) you developed earlier, choose your evidence and plan your commentary. For each solution, address the alternative perspectives by examining pros and cons; then, conclude the paragraph with an evaluation of the solution based on your goal. Address alternate perspectives in your argument by using counterarguments: concession, rebuttal, or refutation.

**Introduction**

Explain and contextualize the problem:

Question (establish goal or success criteria):

| **Option One** | **Option Two** | **Option Three** |
|---|---|---|
| **Pros** | **Pros** | **Pros** |
| **Cons/Objections** | **Cons/Objections** | **Cons/Objections** |
| **Evaluation Based on Goal** | **Evaluation Based on Goal** | **Evaluation Based on Goal** |

**Proposed Solution**

Clear and sufficient justification:

Limitations (concession or qualifying language):

**Conclusion**

Description of outcomes and implications:

Thesis:

Call to action:

**Graphic Organizer: Revising and Editing a Problem/Solution Argument (p. 686)**

| Peer Revision Checklist: Revising and Editing a Problem/Solution Argument | | |
|---|---|---|
| **Revising and Editing Checklist** | **Unit 8 Focus Skills** | **Comment on the Effectiveness and/or Make a Suggestion** |
| Does the claim in the introduction or conclusion connect the subject to a perspective? | *Problem-solution argument* | |
| Has the writer explained the problem and connected the solutions to his or her perspective? Are these choices effective for the specific audience and purpose? | *Addressing complexity* | |
| Is the evidence and commentary organized by the possible solutions to the problem? Does the writer evaluate the solutions based on a goal and make a recommendation to the reader? | *Justifying a claim* | |
| Has the writer evaluated the solutions and employed rebuttal, refutation, and/or concession when appropriate? | *Developing a counterargument* | |
| Is the writing clear and specific? Does the word choice convey the writer's attitude toward the subject? Does the writer employ rhetorical comparisons or express irony or incongruity? | *Connecting with an audience through stylistic choices* | |
| Is the writing free of errors in spelling, usage, punctuation, capitalization, and agreement? | *Writing conventions* | |

# UNIT 9

# Joining the Conversation

**Activity Handout: Understanding an Issue (p. 704)**

Think of an existing conversation about an issue that is important to you. In this context, issues are problems or questions within a broader subject: Should we raise the minimum wage? Should college athletes be paid? How should we protect endangered animal species? How much weight should be given to standardized test scores in the college admissions process? Of course, many others have addressed these questions before you, so you are joining a conversation already in progress. Choose an issue that is important to you. Then use the following graphic organizer to help deepen your understanding of both the issue and the wider conversation.

| **Joining the Conversation: Understanding an Issue** | | |
|---|---|---|
| | **Questions to Consider** | **Your Notes and Comments** |
| **Subject** | What is the topic or issue? | |
| **Significance** | Who cares about it? Why? | |
| **Perspective** | What perspective do you currently have about the subject or issue?<br><br>Why do you have that perspective?<br><br>What biases do you have? | |
| **Other Perspectives** | What other positions and/or perspectives exist about the subject?<br><br>What are others' arguments about the subject?<br><br>Has this subject been addressed before? When? Where?<br><br>Which arguments do you agree with? Why?<br><br>Which ones do you disagree with? Why? | |

| | | |
|---|---|---|
| **Position** | What is your position and perspective about the subject? | |
| **Response** | Who will agree with you?<br><br>Who will corroborate your position?<br><br>Who will be the skeptics or disagree with your position? Why? | |
| **Implications** | How will your position affect others?<br><br>How will this response affect future audiences?<br><br>What are the short- and long-term consequences? | |

**Graphic Organizer: Understanding the Rhetorical Situation (p. 706)**

As you read Crenshaw's Veterans Day address, consider how he reveals his understanding of different perspectives. Use the following graphic organizer to record textual evidence.

| Joining the Conversation: Understanding Perspectives | | |
|---|---|---|
| | **Questions to Consider** | **Evidence from the Text** |
| **Subject** | What is the topic or issue? | |
| **Significance** | Who cares about it? Why? | |
| **Perspective** | What perspective does the writer have about the subject?<br><br>Why does he or she have that perspective?<br><br>What biases might he or she have? | |
| **Other Perspectives** | What other positions and/or perspectives exist about the subject?<br><br>What are others' arguments about the subject?<br><br>Has this subject been addressed before? When? Where? | |
| **Position** | What is the writer's claim (position, perspective, and idea) about the subject? | |

| **Response** | Who corroborates or agrees with the writer's claim? Why?<br><br>Who disagrees with or is a skeptic of the writer's claim? Why?<br><br>Who doesn't care either way? | |
|---|---|---|
| **Implications** | How could the writer's claim or conclusion affect others?<br><br>How will the writer's response affect future audiences?<br><br>What are the short- and long-term consequences of the writer's claim or conclusion? | |

**Activity Handout: Responding to Others' Arguments (p. 713)**

Consider the following claim: "To ensure the safety and privacy of our students, minors should have absolutely no unmoderated access to the internet (including use of social media, streaming videos, online gaming, and chat rooms)."

Identify examples of evidence you could use to corroborate, refute, rebut, or concede to the preceding claim.

| Purpose of Evidence | Definition | Examples of Evidence |
|---|---|---|
| **Corroboration** | Uses evidence or sources that complement or support an argument | |
| **Refutation** | Demonstrates with evidence that all (or a portion) of a competing claim is invalid | |
| **Concession** | Accepts all (or a portion) of a competing claim as correct or correct under different circumstances | |
| **Rebuttal** | Offers a contrasting perspective on an argument and its evidence, or provides alternative evidence to propose that all (or a portion) of a competing claim is invalid | |

**Graphic Organizer: Analyzing the Purpose and Effect of Evidence (p. 715)**

As you read Williams's argument, record specific moments when he uses evidence to address the perspectives of others. After identifying these examples, explain the effects of each piece of evidence within his argument.

| Analyzing the Purpose and Effect of Evidence | | |
|---|---|---|
| **Purpose of Evidence** | **Example(s) from the Text** | **Effect of Evidence** |
| **Corroboration** | | |
| **Refutation** | | |
| **Concession** | | |
| **Rebuttal** | | |

**Activity Handout: Determining a Rhetorical Strategy (p. 724)**

Think of a conversation about an important subject that you've had recently or would like to have. You can also choose one of the following:

• Working a summer job while in high school
• Using the ACT or SAT as part of the college admissions process
• Reducing your carbon footprint
• Playing a sport or being active in a club while in high school
• Participating in a service-learning initiative
• Spending time with (or caring for) family members

Identify your claim (idea + perspective). Then use the following organizer to outline a possible argument that draws upon multiple methods of development to connect with your audience, justify your claim, and achieve your purpose.

| **Subject:**<br><br>**Claim:** | | |
|---|---|---|
| **Your Strategy** | **Method of Development** | **Intended Effect** |
| | | |
| | | |
| | | |
| | | |
| | | |

**Graphic Organizer: Analyzing the Organization and Development of an Argument (p. 725)**

As you read "It's All a Part of the Game," use the following table to capture how Barry arranges and organizes his argument. Then explain how these strategic choices contribute to his purpose and justify his claim.

| **Claim:** | | |
|---|---|---|
| **Writer's Strategy** | **Method of Development** | **Intended Effect** |
| | | |
| | | |
| | | |
| | | |
| | | |

**Activity Handout: Analyzing a Writer's Style (p. 731)**

Find an advertisement (either digital or print) that draws upon the elements of style discussed in this chapter. Then describe the details of the ad and explain how the rhetorical choice contributes to the purpose of the text and the audience's understanding of the message.

| Element of Style | Detail from the Ad | Explain How the Rhetorical Choice Contributes to Purpose and Meaning |
|---|---|---|
| **Diction** | | |
| **Syntax** | | |
| **Punctuation** | | |
| **Design Features** | | |

**Graphic Organizer: Analyzing How Stylistic Choices Enhance Meaning (p. 732)**

As you read Geerken's essay, pay attention to her rhetorical and stylistic choices. Use the organizer to identify some of the ways that her style contributes to her purpose.

| Analyzing How Stylistic Choices Enhance Meaning | | |
|---|---|---|
| **Element of Style** | **Examples from the Text** | **Contribution to Purpose and Message** |
| **Diction** | | |
| **Syntax** | | |
| **Punctuation** | | |
| **Design Features** | | |

**Graphic Organizer: Acknowledging Multiple Perspectives (p. 774)**

Consider the specific rhetorical situation of your argument. Then answer the following questions about your issue as you prepare to write your multimodal argument.

| **Joining the Conversation: Understanding an Issue** | | |
|---|---|---|
| | **Questions to Consider** | **Notes and Comments** |
| **Subject** | What is your topic or issue? | |
| **Significance** | Who cares about it? Why? | |
| **Perspective** | What is your current perspective on the subject?<br><br>Why do you have that perspective?<br><br>What biases do you have? | |
| **Other Perspectives** | What other positions and/or perspectives exist about the subject?<br><br>What are others' arguments about the subject?<br><br>Has this subject been addressed before? When? Where?<br><br>Which arguments do you agree with? Why?<br><br>Which ones do you disagree with? Why? | (Summarize, Paraphrase, Quote) |
| **Position** | What is your position and perspective about the issue or subject? | |

| **Response** | Who will agree with you?<br><br>Who will corroborate your position?<br><br>Who will doubt or disagree with your position? Why? | (Refutation, Concession, Rebuttal) |
|---|---|---|
| **Implications** | How will your position affect others?<br><br>How will this response affect future audiences?<br><br>What are the short- and long-term consequences? | |

**Activity Handout: Unifying Your Argument across Multiple Methods of Development (p. 778)**

To achieve your purpose, you will need to determine the needs and values of your audience. Then you will need to meet those needs. Use the following chart to plan your line of reasoning. Include at least two different methods of development and explain your choices.

| Part of the Argument | Method(s) of Development | Purpose or Desired Effect |
|---|---|---|
| Introduction:<br>Context of the argument:<br>Multiple perspectives:<br>Thesis or question to consider: | | |
| Reason 1:<br>Body paragraph: | | |
| Reason 2:<br>Body paragraph: | | |
| Reason 3:<br>Body paragraph: | | |
| Conclusion: | | |

**Activity Handout: Synthesizing Evidence (p. 780)**

• Prepare to write your multimodal argument by selecting evidence that supports your line of reasoning and your claim.
• Include evidence for corroboration, as well as refutation, rebuttal, and/or concession. (Note: you may not have a counterargument in every body paragraph.)
• Record your choices in the following chart. When you have completed your outline, evaluate any apparent biases and limitations of your argument.

| **Thesis (idea + perspective):** | | |
|---|---|---|
| **Reason 1:** | **Reason 2:** | **Reason 3:** |
| Evidence for support | Evidence for support | Evidence for support |
| Commentary | Commentary | Commentary |
| Evidence from alternative perspective | Evidence from alternative perspective | Evidence from alternative perspective |
| Commentary | Commentary | Commentary |

**Graphic Organizer: Revising and Editing a Multimodal Argument (p. 784)**

| Peer Revision Checklist: Revising and Editing a Multimodal Argument | | |
|---|---|---|
| **Questions to Consider** | **Unit 9 Focus Skills** | **Comment on the Effectiveness and/or Make a Suggestion** |
| Does the introduction address multiple perspectives or changing perspectives over time?<br><br>Does the claim in the introduction or conclusion connect the subject to the writer's perspective? | *Acknowledging multiple perspectives* | |
| Has the writer used two or more methods of development in the argument?<br><br>Are these choices effective for the specific audience and purpose? | *Multimodal argument* | |
| **Questions to Consider** | **Unit 9 Focus Skills** | **Comment on the Effectiveness and/or Make a Suggestion** |
| Does the writer incorporate multiple sources of evidence that support the argument?<br><br>Has the writer included evidence from alternative perspectives by employing rebuttal, refutation, and/or concession when appropriate? | *Synthesizing evidence* | |

| | | |
|---|---|---|
| Is the writing clear and specific? Does the word choice convey the writer's attitude toward the subject?<br><br>Does the writer employ patterns of diction, syntax, or other rhetorical choices to create a style? | *Employing voice and style* | |
| Is the writing free of errors in spelling, usage, punctuation, capitalization, and agreement? | *Writing conventions* | |